PRAIRIE JOURNEY

MADELINE COOPSAMMY

TSAR BOOKS

52/5/4

We acknowledge the support of the Canada Council for the Arts
for our publishing program.
We also acknowledge support from the Ontario Arts Council.

Cover design by Michael Crusz

National Library of Canada Cataloguing in Publication

Coopsammy, Madeline F. (Madeline Frances), 1939-
Prairie journey / Madeline Coopsammy.

Poems.
ISBN 1-894770-17-X

I. Title.

PS8605.O66P73 2004   C811'.6   C2004-904848-1

Printed in Canada by Coach House Printing

TSAR Publications
P. O. Box 6996, Station A
Toronto, Ontario M5W 1X7
Canada

www.tsarbooks.com

For my husband, Lloyd, and my children,
David and Eleanor

Contents

Roots

Seasons on the Prairies

Roots

Roots

Rumour had it
that on his deathbed
he sought to make amends
to buy from Heaven
some forgiveness
for the wrong he'd done
and with his worldly wealth
to recompense the daughter
child of the arrowing cane
and indentured servitude
that two-sided coin
of blessing
and of curse

but her young husband
Dravidian blackness intact
forbade his wife
she of the pink cheeks
and aquiline nose
to reclaim her heritage
jewels, property
and name

for generations
they forgot the tale
their pride
would not admit the shame
and when others asked
their awkward questions
they refused to answer
preferring to believe
their fabricated truth

to ignore the tell-tale signs

and wanting no part
of English, Irish, Scot
no admission
of ravishment
of tainted blood
they reverted to
the ancestral name

now searching for roots
they draw a blank
the unknown Britisher
despoiling a line
went to his Maker
unacknowledged
unforgiven

First Hot Dog

Transporting us to the American Main
it disturbed our island sensibilities
with mindless worship of the American dream
infusing into our spare and careful island lives
visions of leather-jacketed teens
in tight-hipped jeans
playing chicken on their highways
or hanging out in derelict cars
at local Soda Shoppes

And the American dream
was Marlon Brando and Jimmy Dean
their sultry-eyed surliness
and fleshy mouths
tearing at the heart-strings
of every teenage island girl
black, white, yellow or brown

wishing for the moon

That day we shared the Dream
in our lean and hungry cafeteria
whose standard fare
of watery juice and sticky "bellyfuls"
never could assuage
the eternal hunger
of growing girls

And as the uniformed chauffeur
in his Nanny's role
unwrapped the long frankfurters
nestled in their beds of

mustard-smeared wax paper
pungent with onions
and watched his three red-haired charges
partaking of their movable feast
squabbling and complaining all the while
for a brief moment our glances locked
the black chauffeur and I
and across the wires
we saw our thoughts
mirrored in each others' eyes
that there were those who ate hot dogs
and those who merely watched.

The Birth of Roti
How to Curry Favor

"The children of Tagore, in funeral shroud
Curry favor and chicken from the crowd."

from Derek Walcott's "The Spoiler's Return"

Parvati was the only one who habitually brought
a curried lunch
packed in a carrier
the kind that only labourers used
and in those conquered islands
where "culture" meant
anything European
ballet and opera
and cucumber sandwiches at tea
her school lunch was despised
derided
the others held their noses while we
the few of us who counted ourselves
lucky to be there
were deeply troubled
that Parvati should
subject herself and us
to this acute humiliation
flaunting our culture
for all the world to see

but soon the others
blacks, whites, Chinese, Syrians
and those whose grandfathers
had overstepped the boundaries

fathering children
the Sociology texts
has never classified
discovered
that though curried roti
smelt something awful
and its tumeric could leave its tell-tale stain
never to be erased
it was food made in Heaven
and now they could be found
queuing up
on Friday nights
in the little roti stalls
which had burgeoned
in the city of Hoosay
in the Main Road of St. James
for roti stuffed with
curried chicken
goat
beef
conch
or shrimp
and thus began the curry favouring
our noted Laureate came to write about.

Today our
Roti-loving culture
is everywhere
carried
to the farthest corners
of our multicultural earth
this global village
free-trade zones
the refugee-filled metropolises

of New York, Winnipeg,
London or Miami,

the soft shelled sandwich
oozing curried meat or fish
from whose humble beginnings
on the streets of "Coolie Town"
has now become a household word
not to be confused with
tortillas
 pizzas
 perogies
burritos
 tacos
nor even
naan
or pita bread

But do not expect to find it
where its seeds were sown

In its Motherland
the curry-scented sub-continent

It was created
on an island
by its children
yearning for their homeland.

King Corbeau

For Freddie Kissoon
Playwright of the People

Our fierce and ungrammatical tongue
having been plucked from us
it was supplanted with the fine and cultured accents
of our English masters
the musical rhythms of
our Irish tutors

you alone above the crowd
strove to elevate
the dialect of our people
to carve a hero
from unheroic matter
your King you imbued
with magisterial greatness
and with all the accoutrements
of a Broadway musical
you built an epic
in a homespun style.

One day atop the lonely Fort George hill
not yet deployed into a tourist Mecca
or retreat from suburbia
buoyed by the effervescent Trades
sentinelled by the pre-historic cannons
monuments of our bloody past
of conquest, defeat, miscegenation, exploitation
and the middle passages of Slavery and Indentureship
you who bear within you
the legacies of both

9

revealed to us, wide-eyed and unbelieving
with the green and callous carelessness of youth
the possibilities of a life
circumscribed by Art

Today the vision of the King
who strove in wretched futility
to break colonial bonds
which derided blackness, disability, poverty
inflames my psyche

You led the way.

Maria

Maria

once we sat together
while the morning sun
filtering through the stained-glass
of our church-turned-school
danced arcs of rainbow hues
upon our numbers and our letters

Maria, I saw you on the bus today
I heard that after Standard Five
and you no more than twelve
were married off
he had come from far-off China
and brought to Carib's shores
he was old enough to be your father

Maria, how I envied
your skill with numbers
the art within your neat and careful script
I thought one day

the law or medicine
would be your calling

Maria, I tried to talk
but you hurried on
into the large white house
but why the sorrow and the tints of blue

beneath the yellow skin?

Maria, I've thought about you often
through the long grey years
and hoped in vain
for childhood's rainbow hues
to dance upon us still.

Corner Park and St Vincent, Circa 1950

Each day I passed her on my way to school
a girl no older than I was
yet she wore the pain of womanhood.
upon her upturned coca-cola crate she sat
as if in wait for me.
But when I sought
a smile
a gleam of friendliness
a sullen and unyielding stare was her response
I flinched to see the bitterness and scorn
that lay beneath the mask she wore
the anguish and defeat within the eyes
I had never seen in one so young.
Beyond the crumbling doorway
of the fort-like ruins
I glimpsed the life within
as dismal as the ancient catacombs

I began to fear her presence as the days went by
my Convent uniform
as shapeless as the cotton dress
that hung about her
mocked her with its badge of privilege
for while I skipped into a world
of light and laughter
she slouched within
the cold stone walls
of her dark and narrow world.

Her image stayed with me all day
and haunted me with questions
that I dared not answer.

Grenada

Grande Anse beach
one April night so long ago
was soft and young
and promising
while time stood still

But Grande Anse beach
limitless stretch of Paradise
reverenced jewel
in our spice - crowned
island of the west
was doomed to
ravishment and near annihilation
caught in the crossfire
of the power play of nations

On Grande Anse beach
so many aeons now
a motley crew
wanderers and searchers
shared its dreams
one April night
so long ago

crowded in military fatigues
guns aloft and blazing
they sought to bring a peace
unrequested and since derided

and Grande Anse beach
stood wistfully forsaken
abandoned

long after they were gone

and abandoning our dreams
our lives took different paths
but forever blessed
by crystal of moonlight
starlight of gold
and drum rolls of waves
upon a midnight shore

Grande Anse beach
One April night
So long ago

Post-Independence

Half of the country
has forgotten how
it used to live
while the other half has never known
freedom from the gnawing hurt of want
and the grimy round of day is capped
with the admen's visions of
the black and beautiful
lounging on their Sunday patios
sipping in the golden glow of evening
and seated in our over-heated carrels
we wonder why
half of the country
has forgotten how
it used to live

Time was when we boasted that we
of Iere's fabled shore
lived brighter than the humming-birds
from fete to fete we flitted
but now our fetes are filled with strays
yelping and scratching
to salvage what they can for nothing
want has made us snarl
half of the country
has forgotten how
it used to live

Tomorrow we will walk the streets
with heads held high
and boast about the fete we bum' last night
the woman we take from the man

who wasn't looking
and the days to come when
the envy chokes us
as we hear about de fellah who
come down from the States on holiday
and how he making money like we
wanting it

we'll cuss and swear awhile
and talk about the good ol' days
and look around and wonder why
half of the country
has forgotten how
it used to live.

Sister

That night she called my name
there in the room we four had shared
and waking to reply
recalled only
the searing truth

for it was after the tears
the screams of shock and horror

after the neighbours had come and gone
the Doctor and the Priest

and it was after the long night of the Wake
the small house overflowing with mourners
people we hardly knew
vendors from the Main Road
a place to which we ventured only
to procure the necessities of life
the sugar, salt and Hops bread
the smoke herring, salted cod from Canada
the salami and cheese from Italy
the ribbons, needles and thread
from which we wove
the home-made fabric of our lives

and I recall
resentment, anger
at the temerity, the insensitivity
of a neighbour's son
who regaled us with tales of
absurdity and foolhardiness
to which I, too, laughed wholeheartedly

only to endure, afterwards
a deep and purple shame

It was only later
after centuries it seems
among a Northern race
in a cold and vicious clime
where mourning is formalized, circumspect
dignified
that I understood
the kindness
the folk wisdom of my people
island people
who knew better than to
leave us alone
to mourn our dead in peace.

But why she called that night
I'll never know
and though the years have washed us
clean of tears
the memories remain
as fresh as yesterday

the kimono from Madame Butterfly

The Bohemian Girl
trilling her Visions of Marble Halls

a wedding dress of tulle

a sister's love.

Memoir

The night Mahatma was assasinated
a continent away
I walked alone at twilight
through city streets I knew so well
and yet I peered in every alley way
fearing that a gunman lay
behind each bush, each darkening shadow
and I felt a chill although the Tropic night was warm

Naomi:
Woman Lost

Ancestral voices called to her
across Atlantic waters
echoing on her lonely hill
beneath Caribbean skies
and this woman wrapped in jute
her shoulders bare
hair its natural Afro
always smiled benignly
when we came to see her
city children borne like magnet
to the tapia hut
to say, "Morning, Naomi,"
"Morning, children," was all she said
"She eats her hair," the children whispered,
"though we always leave her food."
And they were proud to show us
this enigma of their hills
and the parents grimly said,
"She was a teacher, once, you know,
until somebody's obeah 'did' for her
they "put her so."
Deep within the forest's silences
its rain-damped earth and tangling creeper
far from the ebb and shout
of island waves
Naomi listened to the river's
muted symphony
and said,
"I'll eat my hair
and wear the robes of my ancestors
and spit upon your world."

But she was wiser than we knew
this woman of the hills
no bag-burdened lady
of the streets she'd be
in dignity and emptiness
she found another way
until one day
we looked in vain for her
and I, bereft,
wondered why
the ajoupa, too, was gone
no memory left
no shrine remaining
to Naomi
lost woman of the hills.

Daybassie

He comes to me in dreams
now patient, wise, forgiving
Sadhu, Guru, man of peace
he who was once an untamed spirit
of wild and hoary locks
seeking in vain
his place in that new land
locked in silence
in his native tongue
trailing memories of Mother Ganga

Daybassie milked the cows
and brought them home
from that very common
where the Muslimeen
now hold their fort
and veil their women
and thought to test their strength.
The grazing common now no more
the city has outlawed the cows, the horses
and the ducks and chickens
in the backyards of the houses
of what was once called "Coolie Town"
Daybassie's spirit
lives only in my dreams
wherein he counsels me
as I, now dumb,
trailing memories of "Coolie Town"
try to reconcile two worlds
as Daybassie
Nirvana now attained
smiles in wisdom and in glory.

Seasons on the Prairies

Immigrant

I see her every day
crossing the parking lot at four,
a black anomaly within a land of snow,

A lonely and misplaced woman
desperately squeezing from the land
its celluloid comforts.

Caribbean temper chilled
by guarded hostile looks
that stop the blood more than the blizzards and the frosts
of barren Prairie winters,
she often wonders Why.

Not slave, neither ayah nor domestic
but now as pedagogue she comes.
wistfully seeking a better life.

To Canada, land of silver dreams,
refuge of slave, reject and persecuted.
But when the dross of mass-produced
catalogue-bought trifles
has worn,
and when the shiny metallic coach
has spluttered and groaned its last
somewhere upon a lonely highway
its guts congealed by biting cold,
and when the sun petulantly hides its head,

then insane jungle rhythms reverberate from
the gaudy Hilton perched crazily upon the
Belmont Hills

and amidst the fevered tingle of rum punches
Carnival spectres arise from
decaying Baronial mansions around the
Queen's Park Savannah
and return to haunt her.

The Second Migration

Was it the bloody-minded Kali
or the many-handed Shiva
who thought it fit to lead us
from the green wastes of the Indo-Gangetic
to the sweet swards of the Caroni
then in a new migration
to Manitoba's alien corn?
They never thought to state
the price to be exacted
or how or where it should be paid.
Images of a just society dangled
tantalizingly before our eyes
we thought that here at last and now at last
the spectres of colour
would never haunt
our work, our children's lives, our play
that in the many-faceted mosaic, we -
angled and trimmed to fit -
were sure to find ourselves
our corner of the earth.
How could we not know
that time, which heals
just as frequently destroys
and like the sixties' flower darlings
we, too, must soon become anachronisms
reminders of a time
a time of joy and greening.
We are the mistakes of a liberal time,
you did not really court us, it is true
rather, purging us with neon-coloured pills of
medicals and points and two official languages
your tolerant humanity

festered woundings of "brain drain,"
while our leaders pleaded, impotent in agony
"Do not take our best!"

"We want your best,
No Notting hills for us," you warned.
So once again we crossed an ocean
convinced that little Notting Hills we'd never be.

Now lounging in our bite-sized backyards
and pretending that we do not see
the curling vapours of our neighbour's burger feast
(the third this week)
borne on the Prairie wind across the picket fence
we ask ourselves how far we are
from San Juan, Belmont and St James.

For My Daughter

Cradling your soft cheek
I think about the poets
who have enshrined
their immortal daughters
within their lyric lines
and know that neither mother love
nor mother prayers
will ever stay the drift of tides
or thwart the hurricane or blizzard
from its ordained path
that though today we wrest
with punctuation
and with
the wonderment of numbers
the cycle has begun
and though I strive to hold you
from the untoward
hands of fate
perhaps you too
will one day turn from me
as I have turned from her
the one who bore me
and that someday
as she, my mother sits and waits
in her heat-encrusted cocoon
waiting for the evening
and the cooling Trades
to bring release from day's
too wearisome round
catching the dying moments of life's short
joys
will I too wait

safe in my Prairie cocoon
while my daughter
treads her life within Manhattan's dizzy mazes
or rides the surf in California sun
And I, despairing and disheartened
assail the Heavens with my prayers
as now she does for me?
as she has done
through nights when she, unknown to me
was ever watching
as I battered on the Shakespeare texts
unfurled the mysteries of conjugations and declensions
and she, not knowing what I had to know
yet waiting, always waiting,
was there to fill the cocoa cups
to mend and starch virginal blouses
and the fading Convent tunics
and all the while believing
that one day I, the favored daughter
would bring an honour to her house
which honour yet is still to come
but for her patience and her faith
I can only ask, for you, my own
the honour I have yet   to find.

Hybrids

Only the strong survived
the bitter crossing
their children's children
never spoke of it
in the suburban homes
far from the rural roots
of indentured immigration
the barrack-yards
of the sugar-cane plantations.
Instead we saw them learn
to survive
beginnings
a new religion
embraced to earn
a British education.

Not for themselves
they cast away
goddess worship
or the thousand gods of Hinduism
but for their children
exhorting them
to revere
the crucifixes
and forsaking Pujas
to keep the Lent instead
exchanged their orhinis
for English hats
and later
Spanish-style mantillas
until the Church decreed

all women's headgear
obsolete

now we too
have learnt our own survival
adrift
in snowy northern wastes
or on the hard-edged pavements
of New-World cities
bearing within us
ancestral memories
of two rejected cultures
have bred a generation
hardened to survive a third.

Happy Days

We are a lost generation
we island children of the fifties
who sought to make our marks
upon a foreign soil
and some of us now lie interred
on strangers' land.

Seduced by images, mythologies
of our multi-cultured
    conquistadores

we fled to London,

    Toronto, Boston
thirsting to make their art,
    their icons,
their symphonies
    our own.

Now every white
hoary-crusted December
we find
    our lost sunscapes
our myriad blues
    of sea and sky
the sensuous grandeur
    of our rain-forested hillslopes
warmed by the fervid music
    of our ancestral drums
are bartered now
    to the highest bidder

who revere
the cultural wastelands
that we squandered
while we

ekeing out
subsistence wages
from the inhospitable beds
of these northern climes
now look on

in consternation.

In the Dungeon of My Skin

In Suez they thought I was Egyptian
In Manitoba they wonder if I'm native-born
In India they said derisively:
Indian Christian! Goan! Anglo-Indian!
In the Bronx, wayside vendors spoke to me
in the guttural music of Cervantes and Borges.
A long time ago, in my native place
on coral shores beside the Pirates' Main
they said, "You surely must be Spanish."
In a country famous for its indiscriminate racial copulation
ethnic nomenclature was the order of the day
and "Spanish"
was a mantle that gathered in its folds
all who bore or seemed to bear some trace,
however faint, of European ancestry.
It labelled you a cut above
the blacks and Hindus, low men on the totem pole;
rendered you a more pleasing place in the racial mosaic.

Now though the landscape of my being
negates the burnished faces of my youth
while molten rhythms
forged from the heart of Africa and India
elude me now
and I have cast from consciousness
satiric folk-songs spawned from the tortured metres of our
bastard English tongue
have clipped the bonds of cultures and boundaries
and made myself a universal woman
yet this poor frame, no castle
proves itself no fortress, but a dungeon from which
there can be no release.

Invisible Woman

Invisible Woman
                you have to serve
your time
                why not volunteer
if meaningful activity
is what you seek?
   do not mind that
other hands
    are paid for what they do

Invisible woman
you must forget
     the sweat and tears
that filled the Urn
once called
     a classical education

that was in
another country
     prestigious symbols
of the old world
mean nothing in the new

Invisible woman
                do not strive
for
                commendation
or
acknowledgement

Invisible woman
              can you type?
Parlez-vous Francais?
did your people homestead here?
eat the red dust of
Depression years?
flee from ravaged
Europe?
Discard the 'Skis"
And anglicise their names?

Invisible woman
              though you cannot buy
              a change of skin
You have to serve
              your time.

Subject to Icing

The ominous sign rears its head
as I approach the bridge
distracts me from the task at hand
while my thoughts run on
to white-swathed tiers of
wedding cakes
with pink-tipped rosebuds subtly peeping
exuding the faint-sweet scent of almonds
and memories of children's birthday cakes
lovingly smeared with seven-minute icing
or slithery surfaces of simple butter icing
come flooding

this is no time
for nostalgic thoughts
of wedding cakes
or celebrations
And so with heart in hand
I cross the bridge
recalling
the first time ever
this warning had impaled itself
upon my consciousness

It was beneath Saskatchewan's never-ending skies
in a waterless Summer
and while its land and people
bled in silence
dismissing
not without some guilt
this untimely roadside marker
in thankfulness

I hurried home to Manitoba
only to find
suddenly
these warnings here as well

And I prefer it as it was before
before I took my heart in hand
venturing across the bridges
preferred it
when I did not know
such portents of impending doom existed
liked to think
the care was only mine
in all my epic journeys
across this polar land.

And I muse upon the wisdom
of these merchants of the signs
who sitting in their offices
could conceive of such a line as
"Bridge subject to Icing."
It must have been a man
a woman would have known
that it would never do
would only make one wonder
about consistency and texture
and even
will it ever dry?

"Bridge subject to icing."

Springtime on the Prairies

Sunday mornings
           of a Prairie Spring
when shuttered winter
           is laid to rest
are bright with promise

but the islands
           beckon
and every light
           and lilac-scented breeze
is their siren call
           seducing me
into the open seas
           with Gulf winds at my back
embracing me
           and salty backwash
leaving its
           stinging aftertaste
like some
           forbidden nectar.

Instead I dress for Church
           and return to chores

But other Sunday mornings
           of warm green islands
           cradled
in their tender womb
           of sky-blue sea
have left me

r
e
s
t
l
e
s
s

recalling a risky fisherman's craft
whose temperamental outboard motor
was our passport to another life
where ensconced on Nelson Island
we were one with
sun, sea, sky and wind
ignorant that
this was our own Ellis Island
our ancestors' Quarantine Depot

for our colonial education
celebrated
Toussaint, De las Casas
British Kings and Queens
Vikings, Wellington, Bonaparte
daffodils and Whistler's Mother
but of Indentureship
another kind of slavery,
only a deafening silence.

And though
Prairie Springtime Sunday mornings
hurt and blister
with intimations
of Caribbean Sundays

of a long-departed time
I will not mourn
for I know the loss
is not
for palm-fringed bays
nor cinnamon-scented breezes
but for bronze and perfect bodies

innocence

and

youth.

Keats Did not Live in Manitoba

Keats did not write
of Fall in Manitoba
but on cool September mornings
his season of mists
comes vividly to mind
battling to hold
the white line on the highway
straining to see the murky substance
of the car ahead

on such mornings
Camelot appears
and anything is possible

but in the fields
the vines are fading fast and drying
while the mellow fruitfulness of Summer berries
is but a memory now
and though the good farm wives
husband so carefully
the multitudinous zucchinis
into cakes and loaves
and sometimes marmalade
or even relish too
as I hear tell
the plump and juicy cukes
tomatoes reddened on the vine
wilt and shrivel with the first frost
only the pumpkins remain
cossetted beneath their twisting leaves
awaiting Halloween
and the cheers of children

and on November first
the gruesome jack-o-lanterns
appear somewhat shame-faced
at the curbs
for the BFI compressors
while children in Bosnia
Somalia
and the Rio favelas
are rooting through the dumps
to find a crumb to eat.

Family Is Now

From severed bonds of
family and home
in rain-washed jungles
of equatorial islands
with seasons marked only by
passages of tides
we learn that family
is now
Christian and Jew
once-slave and infidel
and family is now
wherever we can find it
under these Prairie skies

at Summer BBQ'S
or Christmas firesides

now cast adrift from moorings

the rituals of marriage, birth and death
of the extended hordes of cousins
aunts and uncles
who came and went
through open doors
and wind-swept verandahs
we find that family is now
an ethnic group
the immigrant connection
those who
journeying from
their corners of the earth
have braved the seven seas

to put down roots
upon this nurturing soil

and family for us
are all who welcome
our Summer skins
our scented foods
and inviting us
to the harvest and the toil
share with us
the bounty of the table.

Prairie Journey

Sometimes
through the windows of the bus
those shimmering fields of white
assume a new dimension
and deceive me into thinking
that I am once more
on the verandah of my uncle's house
dreaming hourly
as I gaze upon the sea
and the flickering beacons of the distant farms
are really only
twinkling lights
of ships on the horizon
stars which beckoned us
in all their wonder and their beauty
to the worlds beyond the seas.

those seas we've travelled since
while the wonder and the beauty
that we sought
have brought us to
apartment blocks in
decaying inner-cities
suburban ghettoes
where the new west begins
and some of us
to traverse fruitlessly
the unrelenting highways
between our Prairie towns.

The white house
with its overwrapping verandah
in the historic and genteel Mucurapo

has long changed hands
many times over
the ocean view
which was ours
when we had so little else
has been obliterated
by ruthless and indiscriminate
"development"

this residential neighbourhood
once coveted and sought by
those who wished to climb
the ladder of respectability
has now become
a marketplace
grotesque and utilitarian
its edifices soar relentlessly
while we strain futilely to glimpse the
shoreline
to revel in the blue light of the waves
to be soothed by their eternal wash.

For our third-world country
now ceaselessly pursuing
the Yankee dollar
only leaves us decrying
the loss of our heritage
for all that once had nurtured us

To mourn the loss
is futile now
we only have ourselves to blame
for while our children pursued
the North American dream

we left our borders
undefended
the stranger at the Gate has entered
and raped and pillaged
leaving us once more
hewers of wood and drawers of water

we are the new colonials.

The Conquerors

Now hostage to the unrelenting ravages of time
we stand reduced
to virile youth and passive age
the eight-point system learned in youth
of race and colour
master and slave
labourer and overseer
colonizer and colonized
now count no more

once, wearing our knowledge and degrees
with pride and confidence
we stormed the bastions of far-flung continents
to lives and civilizations
we thought to conquer

it counts no more
the lightness of the skin
how finely sculpted face or form
with beauty's lineage
or the symmetry of youth

and these too, count no more
the laurels and the medals

now we, an aging population
with children who fear only
the white-out of the Prairie blizzard
who have never felt
the hurricane's blinding rage
nor witnessed its relentless force
that culls the salt-sprayed coconut palm

from its sandy base
and flings it prostrate into a boiling sea
try in vain to teach
the hard-won lessons we have learned
that our ribboned honours earned
at so much cost
will only be reduced at last
to a tireless drip
through an intravenous jar
the sterility of a nursing station
and the charity of strangers.

Now we are reduced
to a two-point system only
the living and the dying.

Recession and the Third World Immigrant

This honey-flowing milk and maple-syrup land
promised a new beginning.
No longer sure of friend or foe
they fled in hope
and left the victors pecking at the spoils
as Massa's day now done
he lightly shrugged aside his burden.
For the drums no longer summoned them
to bacchanalian joy
but tom-tom like
they throbbed a coming Holocaust.
In despair
like Israelites of old
they fled
to find the promised land.
The land was vast and wide
they knew
but shivered in the throes of its
retreating glacial cover.
Yet when the winter waned
the time of love and joy and corn proved sweet and easy
the natives sang a song of welcome
as moving over gently, they swore
there's room for all.
Gullibly the strangers thought
the promise of the Spring and Summer's opulence
would never fail.
But now the land is vast and wide
and cold
suspicion, fear and envy greet them
from the Circle to the Island
The land is bone
Will this Winter of opprobrium, doubt & discord never end?

Spring Song in a Land of Endless Summer

For Barbara Who Sang

Your glorious accents quavering and rising
to the richness of that song of Spring
you suffused our one-room school
with a melody as full-throated
as that of the returning birds of Spring
while trilling rivulets of June
ran past the sterile asphalt
of our city school yard
and in that land of endless Summer
as we chanted verses
memorized our tables and our sums
our senses spun
fed by a poet's tome
his joyful visions
of a world awakening

this world has come and now is almost gone
the rivulets of years
have washed away
those eager melodies
that filled my soul with joy
and fed my hopes and dreams

today whenever June is here
in my land of endless winter
I wish for you
a world as new and fresh
filled with the endless possibilities
of June
as that you gave to us
so long ago.

Lost Gypsy

No babushka this
the multicoloured scarf
she sports with style and grace
framing a face of timeless bones
now cured into the finest Prairie leather
and from the corners of the perfect mouth
a smile seems always lurking

on better days I've seen her
push an ancient bicycle through town
while at other times
she wields the ignominious
long and pointed stick
borne by those on city welfare
who earn their keep
scavenging the wastes
of those more fortunate than they

and yet this worn and tattered personage
exudes intimations
of other times and other places
images of gypsy caravans
which once had crossed the seas
and left behind
a wandering child
who merges now into a universal sisterhood
indistinguishable from the native-born
to roam still free and unattached
to no one but herself

Winnipeg Summer

Her Summer loveliness
is dull and orderly

From suburban concrete jungles
to the river's gabled glories
her short-lived Summer joys
leave no room for despair
from vulgar gaze her shaded avenues
protect petunaied planters
mellow in their puny blaze

Winnipeg Summer beauty
like the Red and ribboned river
crescendos to majestic glory
ignoring
in her smug benevolence
the darker side of life

no squalor, mystery or dirt
besmirch her face
unless to Main Street
where the others say "they" live
the drunks and vagrants
who lie outside Salvation's pale

and in front of City Hall
the old men sun

But at one a.m.
while the City Fathers sleep
visions of world-class cities
shoring up their dreams

Main Street spawns its life
a bouncer cracks a fist
and with a snow-plow's crushing arms
seizes and lifts its victim
as though to
disembowell it
within its cavernous maw
but instead
spews it out
onto the sidewalk

The Patrol car draws up
in righteous indignation
But Winnipeg summer beauty

is dull and orderly.

The Passing Show

The snow makes faery patterns
across the highway
but I dare not lose myself
with wild imaginings
plowing straight ahead
hands frozen to the wheel
I watch for lines
which often disappear
and pray
that I might keep the speed
before the lumbering beast
some flame-belching
pre-historic monster
attempts to pass
and blow me off my course
or blanket me
beneath the snow
it's bound to leave
within its wake

but ever so often
another threat is bound to loom
a patch of slippery
uncompromising ice
fit for figure skaters
and the hockey Titans
but not for vulnerable
mid-sized sedans

my life will flash before me soon

Manitoba

winter driving

Prairie Seasons

Once more the land has changed
from green to gold to brown
and as the Summer splendor fades
and Autumn glories are denuded
the spirit too
like prairie soil
assumes an iron-hard dimension
bracing for the bitter onslaught
of another cruel season
couched in her shroud of deathly white
the ennui of winter sameness
except when
in a maddened rage
her savage winds
assail the man-made comforts
we have carved from Prairie wilderness

now youthful strength
and carefree optimism fading
the weight of winter
becomes a thought too hard to bear
for unlike the stalwart evergreens
who wear with grace their burden
of the winter white
and unlike earth's buried promise of the Spring
I, cracked and broken
will never see rebirth
and bowed and humbled
as I watch the Autumn colours
and the Summer's memories recede
fear the heavy yoke of one more Winter
and cry, "No more, no more!"

Spring Returns to Portage and Memorial

All Winter long I wept
because I could not leave
I longed to see the Prairie fields
encased in snow
and leave behind this grime and gray of city streets

but now that Spring is here
this mean and ugly stone
has magically been transformed
to castles brave
and fortresses of light
on which the winds blow clear and free

and city streets too long encrypted
in Winter's funereal shroud
now lie naked to the sun.

And now I do not want to leave.

Patterns

Time of darkness
time of hopelessness
milestones reached
time in which
all fears and dark dreams
have realized themselves
time to wonder and consider
choices made
and places lost
patterns which
repeat themselves
to ennui and futility
time of helplessness
as forces, tides and winds
now buffet us
questions still unanswered
the strong displace the weak
youth and strength
too soon diminishing
a world in chaos
comforts won
now being lost too fast
and old age
with its own excuses
still too far away
blankness, emptiness, whiteness
where are the friends we loved
the faces of our youth
the promises that life
now
mocks us with?
the faces of our children

question us in fear
we have no answers
no comforts
for our own are lost

Ode to a Pencil

For My Inner City Students

This brown and wasted implement
has fought a thousand wars
its once-bright armour
now cracked and worn beyond repair
its sword-point non-existent
this pathetic relic, once revered
can no longer enter into battle

frankly, my child, this is a non-pencil.

Coffee, Tobacco, Pepper and Rum

How subtly they insinuate themselves
into our beings
luring us to Kingdoms which are nameless
lethal substances eliciting from us
highs that cannot be classified, labelled, catalogued,
analysed, categorized, explained, dismissed

and when gleefully we travel
to famed and distant outports
viewing monuments of grandeur
fraught with history
echoing from their ramparts
with the footsteps of the tyrants, Kings
and conquistadores
who levelled all before them
in the name of Empire
or misplaced Glory to some Almighty being
standing at Stonehenge
ogling at Versailles
revelling in the fabled glory of
the sidewalks of Montparnasse
exulting
to be here at last

We wonder

Has anyone yet classified, labelled,
catalogued, analysed, categorized, explained or dismissed
such exhilaration that is felt?

And what of music
that resonates deep within us

impelling us to laugh and sing and dance
in some transport of bacchanalian revelry?
Or books that stir
deluding us for some little while
we too have seen Heathcliff on the moors

Have these too, ever had a designation?
a local habitation and a name?

Or gourmet feasts
studded with the purple grape
subtly graced with plundered spices
of the aromatic east

Such highs
Have they ever been
classified, labelled, catalogued, analysed
categorized, explained, dismissed

Coffee, tobacco, pepper and rum.
Only for those who wish to travel
to the realms of gold.

Duel

I have seen the face of racism
looked into his pale blue eyes
and trembled with a fear
inbred from centuries
of domination

his face is white and male
the duelling grounds
on which we meet
are his alone
my weapons only those
that he allows

and if by chance
I were to find some strength
some puny power
unknown and unaccessed before
I will soon be wrested down
left cowering in the dust
or fainting in the dew
 and though I know that
fainting is for pale
and shrinking maids
of centuries long ago
and not for women
of my race
or class
or time

yet I know that
City Hall is strong

and white and male

I cannot win.

Nelly Dean, Nelly Dean

Where did he come from
The little dark thing
harboured by a good man
to his bane?
So had you mused towards the end
Nelly Dean, Nelly Dean
for you had watched it all
as they danced their
macabre steps
upon the treacherous moors
that lay between their Houses.

Often it is you I think of
Nelly Dean, Nelly Dean
sitting solitary at your kitchen fire
savouring the rich scent
of the heating spices
while outside your peaceful sanctum
the wilful gentry
are careening crazily
on their self-destructive course
fuelled by a love and lust
which even death could not release

Did you never feel
Nelly Dean, Nelly Dean
some girlhood yearnings of your own
an urgent need
for someone who was yours alone
who would assuage the cares
those debilitating passions of your betters
laid on you?

In another life you might have been
a wise and gifted teacher
a counsellor, psychologist
for at Heathcliff's envy
of Edgar's golden locks
you craftily wove for him
a noble parentage
his mother an Indian Queen
his father the Emperor of China

for you were sister, mother, nursemaid
though never wife or lover
Nelly Dean, Nelly Dean

You must have been a voyeur
Nelly Dean, Nelly Dean
to enjoy so heartily
the sexual escapades
you narrate with such felicity

And when the snow winds
howl upon my Prairie wilderness
I hear them battering
your fortress on the Heights
see the stunted firs
the gaunt thorns
stretching thirstily towards the sun
and remember you
Nelly Dean, Nelly Dean

Though Lockwood swears
no ghosts can walk
that quiet earth

the fires of the thwarted lovers
have not been quenched
as you who lived it all vicariously
must know too well
Nelly Dean, Nelly Dean.

INDIAN
SOJOURN

Delhi

It was a glorious time
we lived a lie

Through Delhi's ancient streets
we walked at twilight
youth was on our side
and the promise of tomorrow

on every corner
ragged urchins
ply their trade
of threaded jasmine blossoms
to adorn the hair
the wrist
the leprous woman and her child
cry out plaintively
"memsahib, paise do!"
the woman and her escort never hear
the golden sari sweeps by
the bangles jingle
her high-heeled chappals lash the stones

and we too, moved on
into the plushly scented
evening rooms
where fading Anglo-Indian beauties
belt out tunes of yesteryear
synchronising to the rhythms
of the sad-eyed weary Goans
their stock-in-trade
three-piece nightclub bands.

and campus privileged
reliving glory days
of cricket fields and halls
of British public schools
nestled in Himalyan passes
in British Indian slang
attired in pukka Indian garb
ape Village beatniks
and think the west
is all the world there is

and we, too, lived a lie
where Afric's jungles
and Carib's fertile lands
were ours to be conquered
we could not wait
to find our way
seated on a grimy coffee bench
within the narrow compounds
of the red-walled city
or in the cut-glass crystal
of Kashmiri evenings
all of us forgot

dreaming

we saw our lands
baked in nostalgia
and forgot the tribal warfare
ethnic hatreds
the small tin gods
that we had left behind

"the east", we sniffed in scorn

and so we went back
to the worlds we'd left
and some of us to
civil unrest exploding into
ethnic bloodbaths
borders realigned
new countries formed
and we found ours
always verging on
civil war
a threat of battle lines
drawn along racial lines
our only salvation
the annual Carnival
which melted all
into a frenzied potpourri
of bacchanal and sex
and colour and abandon
celebrating the pleasures of the flesh

what price freedom
we ask our small tin gods
who never answer
frantic to reclaim
from tropic opulence
glass and concrete mega-cities
to surpass the metros of the north

once more, a lie
it is a glorious time.

In Memory of Indira Gandhi

I never thought that we would one day mourn
your life cut down by hands
that meant to keep it safe.
Once when you were young and graceful
jewel-toned and silken-sareed
your star still rising
and we were searching for ourselves
you came to tea
a living symbol to the women of our House
of all the undreamed possibilities.
In our ripening years
you rose to power
priestess-like and unadorned
you stood for strength, for women, for survival
a testimony to the psyche
of the namesake and the father
who had molded you.

Autumnal
Season

Au Monsieur Chez Creperie en Montparnasse
To the Gentleman at the Creperie in Montparnasse

Such kind blue eyes
butterfly touch upon my shoulders
meant only to gently move my person
as I waited
for my crepe to sizzle
to be drowned in the ambrosian delight of
a thousand chocolate coated almonds.
And you, needing only a space to stand
to place your order
whispered quietly
"Excusez-moi, madame,"
but I, eschewing now romantic interludes
even in this legendary city
expecting only pickpockets
or worse perhaps
my textbook French not registering quickly enough
your polite request,
turning rudely,
my face expressed
hostility, fear, outrage
and yours
only a puzzled hurt

Soon moving to the other side
viewing quizzically
this aberration of civilization
I saw once more
the blue of your eyes
as deep and clear as my lost ocean depths
plumbing through my rude exterior
vainly trying to explain

wordlessly
you meant no harm
while your face burned
but I
I was afraid to smile,
to apologize

thinking only
this is Paris, 1998,
age is no protection
for a woman alone.

And yet those eyes
their hurt,
sear me even now

Forgive me.

Graymalkin

You came, unbidden and unwanted
to middle-aged complacency
and left a legacy of joy

images remain
ineffectual kitten paws
grasping, as though to hold the world itself
a slippery ball
a noisy rattle
conjuring up the long-forgotten joys of infants
or a fragile stem
mangled from some treasured plant
coaxing us to tolerance

gray perfection
molded into gray upholstery

I comb the matted sideburns
into soft contentment
while gray-green eyes
mellifluous with gratitude
glaze over into bliss

Not in you
the hard-edged strength
needed to survive this world
.

Your life begun in dignity and courage
ended abrubtly
without a hint of farewell
one more turn of the inexorable wheel
of life's injustice

Cat haters labelled you
raccoon, bobcat, child of the woods
but for me
you merited only
Graymalkin
that name whispered by
those weirdest of sisters
on a blasted heath
in a play whose name we dare not say
but merely
"The Scottish play"

Graymalkin .

Maturity

I know now why the old
wear faces and demeanours
I used to scorn

When once you've met
chicanery
        and the cold sneering halls of power
when once you've been bruised and battered
by the sharp and searing laser points
        of greed and selfishness
and in despair realize that
you are powerless to change
the course of ruin they've set you on

trusting lines of youthful beauty
over time erode
into a cynical visage
bored and caustic

yet there is comfort still
        in knowing
        that there is
a higher law

that those who've robbed and cheated
crushed you
        underneath their feet
knowing you have no recourse

will one day have to square accounts
and answer to Him who is
        unwavering, unchanging

and has promised to reward
                    the meek, the mild,
the widows and the orphans.

Ode to Toronto

The windows of my Mayfair room
afford a view of Balboa's Hotel
seducing clients with
Playboy Bunnies
and Miss Nude Toronto
Best V.I.P. In Town

the Towers of Babel
rise in the distance
the staples of our culture
The Bay, CIBC, Manulife Centre
Rogers
their orthogonal symmetry
unrelieved by curvature, ethereal domes
or softening arches
shimmering blue and white
in the setting sun

In the foreground
the spires of a mottled stone Church
loom staid and majestic
their gracious curves and generous green
a fortress of stability of timelessness
mocking the glass and concrete monoliths
monuments to our capitalist gods

Between the Mayfair
and the Sumptuous Suites
a few flat-topped tarpaper roofs
a last testament to the city's past
lie lonely, morose
harbouring the Chinese Take-out

and a Somali eatery
whose unlikely proprietor
turns out to be
a fresh-faced Bangladeshi

Though some decry
the Capitalist crimes
the shallowness and greed
of this our Good and World-class city
even as she takes little mincing steps
trying vainly to outdo
the Joneses of New York
daily the displaced masses of the world
flock through her gates
fleeing fascism, torture
fundamentalism, ethnic cleansing
chauvinism
this secular city-state
a beacon promising
humanism, multiculturalism
freedom, equality
a haven for
the dispossessed
the driven, the homeless
the persecuted.

Toronto The Good.

Prayer

In the incense-riddled glories of the Church
lilies ever-dying on the air
resignation is as easy as a child's first prayer
but when the splendour fades
the organ and the candles both are snuffed
I sit alone.

Teach us, O God, how best to live
sans greed, sans hate
and sans despair

Remembering Evelyn

Evelyn Ste Croix 1945 – 2002
Teacher, Colleague, Friend

I did not want this poem to come
reflected Nobel Laureate Derek Walcott
mourning his friend and fellow poet Eric Roach.
And I too, would not write this poem   .
suppressed and hid it,
fearing it would be
a vain and selfish act

not only will we sorely miss
your countless loving and unselfish deeds
your championship of the rights of all
in public and in private

but your calm and peaceful aura
that quick and eager laugh
which often was
the voice of common sense
challenging the foolish and unreal demands
that were our portion and our cup

ask not for whom the bell tolls
the poet said
and so in selfishness I grieve
for I will miss you, friend

the books we shared
the curried lunches
that we savoured
our musings of right and wrong

of good and evil
you were a rock
on which we all
would rest
to gather strength

there was no clue, no hint
to the end you smiled and shared with us
and kept on giving
of your presence
your warmth and kindliness

and when the poet fails
I turn to Connie Kaldor
warbling of her little Wood River
reminding us that the heart
though bigger than trouble
and bigger than doubt
sometimes needs a little help
to figure that out.

Your parting gift.

Re-Colonization

In Memory of My Uncle
Andrew Mitchell

Now that the rains have come
this July in their appointed time
I marvel at your foresight
in rescuing from wilderness
this little strip of paradise
these lush forested mountain slopes
ablaze with bougainvillea, flamboyant
Hawaiian torch
and a cornucopia of trees
coming to fruition with
papayas, avocados, breadfruit, mangoes
oranges
amidst the harmonious symphony
of a thousand birds

Pursuing immortality
you secured for your descendants
their little patch of earth
but now the world has started
to encroach upon your hill
which once nightly
sparkled tremulously
with scattered evidence of habitation
now shimmers with a hundred pinpricks of light
proclaiming our burgeoning nation's
frantic search for shelter

This mountain fortress
we once mistakenly believed
ours alone

when abandoning the western plains
like conquistadors of old
we forded new rivers
broke new ground

now the plebeians
enclose us from all sides
the estate of the mythical Captain
whom no one ever saw
far above your modest holding
the mountain top
on which we picnicked
sold now to foreigners
for riding stables

your patch of earth
symbolizes our island's fate
our children abandoning their
third world paradise
exchanging it for
prosperity, plastic, glass
cement and bricks

malls

winters of unending despair
while our island people
are colonized again
the conqueror's skin
is still the same
Europe and North America's
sun-starved citizens

for they have paid the piper

while we who deal in ethics
philosophy and pedagogy
have only language
to fall back on

and cry 'foul'

beseeching

no more rape and plunder
of these gentle isles of the Caribees
leave us be
to reap the spoils
of our ancestors' anguish
their chains
passages of indentureship
do not steal once more
our islands' plenty
tropic-burnt produce
dahl-coloured pawpaws
bhagee-green or sunshine-red
zabocas and mangoes

and those no Northern supermarkets
have yet appropriated
sapodillas, chenettes, pomeracs
granadillas, sugarapples,
pommecytheres

they are ours now
we do not wish to share

Tunapuna Market

Through thirty-five years of my wintry exile
the Tunapuna Market
remains unchanged, caught in a time warp
still unspoilt
despite American tv, the Colonel's chicken
those ubiquitous malls
overpriced and overburdened supermarkets
surpassing any in the "developed" world

for some Luddites the old ways
are still the best
and after forty-one years of Independence
this third world anachronism
in our wired world, a mecca for the tourists
is a welcome boon

who dares compare the lives
its purveyors must lead
to those of North American prosperity
we who know first-hand
the loneliness, the starkness
the personal costs of the industrial wasteland
and the dark and arid winters

Here in the Tunapuna Market
such copious abundance
is obscene to us
northerners who wait
longingly
through six drear and hapless months
until the sun dislodges winter's frozen grip
unleashing the rich and careless bounty

of a Manitoba Summer

This island once called home
this blessed Trinite
which the intrepid Columbus
likened to his beloved Valencia
in the Spring
and who was soon dismayed to find
that there were no more islands
left southward
all that remained was
what would be
the debilitating
castration of El Dorado

in this land of eternal Summer
the crowded stalls disgorge
in organized profusion
a plethora of fruits
phallic eggplants purple and sensual
each of its names
more musical than the last
melongene, balangene, bhaigan, aubergine

green onions
in local parlance "chive"
bundled and tied in symmetrical precision
ornamented with tender-leaved
sprigs of pungent thyme
whose aromatic memory
will help sustain us
through many pale and odourless
Sundays of a Manitoba winter.

It is not yet mango season
but the sapodillas are ripe and ready
the brown and white perfection of their
tender succulence equalling
the satisfaction of a million grains
of Caroni sugar-cane
so unlike the green and white
tartness of their Kiwi impersonators

while ruby-red pomeracs
shimmer in the morning sun
the fat brown crabs
once vicious and wild-eyed
lie there defeated
securely fastened at the legs
lest they escape
into the open drains which stream red
with the blood of the slaughtered gutted hens

mundane plantains
earthy homely ground provisions
boasting multi-lingual names
of tannias, eddoes, dasheen, cassavas
lie side by side with
bundles of heart-shaped dasheen bush
tender leafy spinach
bhodi, patchoi and cabbages
soon to be transformed into the culinary delights
of many Sunday tables
surpassing any five-star establishment
which has never known the menus
of bhajee, crab and callalloo

I turn away in scorn from bananas and citrus

94

all too common in the shopping carts
of every first-world shopper
while their third-world harvesters
labour without a living wage
to line the pockets of
their multi-national financiers

I need exotic fruits so long denied me
papayas, yellow, rich and red
tipi-tamboo,
chataigne, our Caribbean chestnut
and Trinidad avocado
its pale-green fleshiness
a sensuous decadence
mocking our memories
of miniscule Florida imports
no bigger than a fist

such equatorial abundance
makes me wary
reflecting on the unrelenting hours
of labour in the scorching sun
which yield such bountiful returns
the fierce and raucous
competition for a customer's attention
for what I surmise is
a paltry recompense
and I wonder what it must be like
at the end of market day
for those whose baskets
overflow with unsold produce
and pockets only half-filled

The Tunapuna market
in January.

The Hills of St Ann's 2002

These graceful spurs and ridges
of the rich and rugged
Northern range
whose bays and inlets
provide retreat and recreation
for all
citizen or foreigner
these hills
eternally green
once meant unfettered days of freedom
a child's idyllic release from
the constraints of city life
daily river jaunts
which yielded mangoes
juicier and sweeter
than any market vendor's city stall

and the indigo joys of unwired Tropic nights
where homeward journeys
down the slippery tumbling hills
were illumined only by flickering flambeaux
an eighteenth century
anachronism in a twentieth century world
magnifying the mysteries
which lay beneath the tangled excess
of our forested daylight wanderings

But today I view these hills
as a symbol of a people's journey
three pioneering families
who with visionary zeal

turned from the frantic progress
of an early twentieth century Caribbean city

Fed by hope and deeply buried memories
of an ancestral past
that led landless starving peasants
of an old and tired East
to be coerced by promises of
a new beginning
in a Brave New Western World
where sugar would be sifted into gold

they carved a hideaway
atop the lonely St Ann's Hills

Now in this second year of the second millennium
fleeing the electronic reality
of our cities and villages
simultaneously decaying beneath
their twenty-first century development
our Highways massed with
the hedonistic excess of luxury vehicles
cumbersome, ungainly SUV's
and the mid-sized sedans of the Proletariat
retreating to our mountainous solace
in Pagan custom
we revere the spirits
of our far-sighted ancestors
eternally present
among the powerful silent sentinels
of this peaceful forested enclave
who continue to oversee and bless
each project, each wistful dream
of their descendants

a grateful tribute
to the creators of this mountain commune

an idea born
before its time.

Carnival 2003

Transplanted Trinis
in various ports of call
strive to replicate
the once-vibrant
art of Carnival and Kaiso
and in the stately streets
of Anglo-Saxon London
Toronto, Edmonton, "The Peg"
they recreate
with nostalgic fervour
the glory days
that once they knew and loved

But in the city of its birth
the art of 'mas is dead
the balladeer's
once-satiric commentary
is old and vile and tired
Spoiler whom Walcott
once equated with
Martial, Juvenal and Pope
is long gone
Kitch is dead
and Sparrow
Calypso King of the World
is quiet
only the Crazies
and the Chi-Chis remain
hastening with their insufferable pens
the downfall of a nation
where murder and kidnapping

the drug-crazed culture of
Miami, New York and Detroit
are the aspirations of our youth
our leaders squabble
posture, and incite the rabble
fracture and ferment us
with racial hatred
but never strive for equable solutions

and on our highways
the shining chariots
badges of success and wealth
are lethal weapons
which daily make our streets run red
with carnage

we need a visionary
another Gandhi, King, Mandela
a man who dares to stand alone
striving for justice, equality
for dignity
and most of all for unity.

Island Sounds

Exiles from our island home
have long revered
the Keskidee's chirp
that irreplaceable memento
of a heritage long lost
while Chanticleer's morning greeting
so long unheard,
forgotten
in the confined regulated
urban winters of our lives
used to be a sound of cheer

yet when the "Qu'est ce qu'il?"
of our beloved Keskidee
and the throaty choruses
of several Chanticleers
vie with the barking of
a hundred village dogs
they serve as startling reminders
that this is still
frontier country
where lawlessness reigns supreme
where building codes
and conflict of interest laws
have yet to be enacted
and in the wake of inhumane
decibel levels of sound
from a neighbouring bar
in the pre-Carnival month
four sleepless week-ends
are shrugged away with
"This is Carnival,"

as Carnival mania
destroys all trace of sanity

In order to survive
men live by their wits
and money talks the loudest
in a land where loud and raucous voices
too often are the norm

After forty-one years of freedom
our politics remain the same
divisive and destructive
forgotten is our once storied past
the accidents of history
which spat us out upon these shores
daring us to peacefully co-exist
in tolerance and harmony
the original multicultural nation

instead

our leaders teach us only
how to hate and fear each other
and in the name of progress,
development at any cost
despising our humble roots
the manacles of slavery
the servitude of indentureship
spurred on by world class
television from First World affluence
we become inured
to murder and corruption
in the high-flying style
of the Mafia Dons

of Chicago and New York.
Our island sounds are now
those of The Sopranos
the screams of fear and outrage
the shotgun blast
as violators of every stripe
and the paid assassins
violently wrest their share
of the fruits of the land.

The Keskidee's cry
whistles from the trees
"What is it? What is it?"

The Mango Tree

A lone and disconcerted lizard still glides
along your partly amputated
bare brown trunk
yesterday he was despairing disconsolate
today he has not found alternative accomodation

only this wounded form remains
of what was once a full and stately
green and flowering mango tree
how much life was sheltered
within your copious verdure
your luxuriant hanging vines
you harboured more than reptilian life

you were a microcosm of the forest

your three-pronged trunk now stands decapitated
reduced to
three amputated limbs
whose wounds lie open raw and white
like the stumps of India's mutilated children
readied for begging for sympathy

No more to be serenaded by
the questioning keskidees
the whistling Blue Jeans
who perched so carelessly
and flitted boundlessly
between your branches
your majestic form

once towered above
the backyard coconuts
of stunted dimensions
insipid bananas and other lesser trees
while the historic breadfruit
your only rival
stood companionably beside you
in quiet harmony

now the naked sun and sky
occupy the space
where once your branches opened
so generously to the world

Today your trunk is now no more

in a neighbourhood
where every empty space
would be a travesty
if not consumed by
miniscule apartments
rentals to the homeless
and the landless
what need is there
for mango trees?

Island Breezes

Island breezes
fragranced zephyrs
cooling scorched and arid landscapes
can never be equated with
Prairie July winds
which madly scatter tumbleweeds
and threaten disaster to
Palliser's triangle
or draughts which cool
Summer's lingering breath
in wistful October nights
warmed by a pumpkin coloured moon
in a northern clime
prefacing winter's frosty birth

Island breezes awaken our soul
chilhood's wondering joys
of evening strolls along our
green historic Savannah
of homeward journeys on
Friday nights from the old Rialto
or the dignified and elegant Roxy
a Mother and two teenagers
basking in the magical after-glow of Hollywood
three women alone
in a safe and simpler time

Island breezes descending
from the Fort George hill
vied with the breezes from the sea at Mucurapo
tempering the overheated Sunday morning services
of the Church of St Mary's

fanned the bodies of the residents
of the House next door
toothless, blind, despairing,
their denim uniforms
tainted with the odious smell of Poverty
seated under the spreading samaan tree
bemoaning their fate
their longevity
or grasping with sinewed claw-like fingers
the chain-link fence
whined to passers-by for alms

Island breezes
were the first unruly stirrings
of adolescent dreams
were whispered promises on
Trade fair nights
on moonlit picnics
at Maracas beach
or on the starlit meadows in hidden valleys
of the northern hills

Island breezes in an open boat
so warm and welcoming
in the dew of the early morning
breathing the subdued excitement
promised by a day of "down the islands"
turned shivery cool and deadly
on a late and terrifying evening journey
ampliflying the crazed uncaring billows
threatening us all with watery grave
a dire warning to inexperienced sailors
of the sea's dominion
its fickle nature and inexorable potency

Island breezes cooled
the heat of writing bodies
the tempo of the kaiso and the pan
at many an outdoor evening fete at Carnival
before they became spectator sports
in the torpor of high noon
and on Carnival Tuesday
while sunshine shimmered on the silk,
the satin and the velvet
of the old-time Carnival
island breezes
rustled the feathers and plumes
of manifold masqueraders
bedecked bejewelled
in costumes intricate and flawless

Island breezes filtering from
the Northern Range
temper the fever of
the over- populated developments
along the east-west corridor
and atop a majestic peak
the Monastery of St Benedict
serene unchanged for ninety years
augmented by the gentle breezes of the heights
stands impassively surveying
the frantic hordes below
pursuing prosperity
first-world status

Island breezes
still bear within their wake
the pensiveness

of temps perdu
still festoon the psyche
with urges and desires
long buried or discarded

Island breezes
have not relinquished
their urgency
their power
to annihalate and shatter
all complacency and smugness
bred from years of cynicism
of disappointment
of acceptance of the human condition
and the loss of eagerness
of hope and all promises of youth.

Song of the Prodigal

Time now
to put away all childish
hopeless dreams

what good now
is all the anxious striving?

The best seller
that will never now be written

little now is left
the decrepit frame is crumbling fast
and all the ills of Job
descend to taunt and harry
the soul in limbo

the visage which clear as day
defines its pock-marked past
its torments, hopes and dreams
so constantly belittled
now wears only bitter resignation

the poets said it all before
life is only a tale of woe
a joke played on those
who dared to take it seriously

and those same poets
the ones who celebrated
truth and beauty
      honour
honesty

and the ethicists
who taught us boastfulness
a crime
where are they now
in our small and meagre scheme

for that was in
another country

we had to learn
new ways to survive this land
to speak a language not our own

this court still harbours
the smiling jester's face
while yet he flings the poisoned barb
into the breast of the vain and flattered king

 But we

commoners, fiefs and peasants all
had none to jibe and jostle
to keep us sane
only each other
to help us weave the fabric of our lives
to shield us from the crimes of social ills
unemployment, welfare, cutbacks
homelessness

while affirmative action
hiring quotas, women's rights
and those of visible and handicapped minorities
all quietly disappeared

and always…

in spite of superhuman effort
batteries ran out, the monitors failed
to be cast into
the junkheap of lives once lived

and health and wealth
the upward mobility
we sought so assiduously
were soon ground into
the destructive tumbling shifting sands
of the backwash of the wave

once we earned with pride
the bungalows, the sprawling splits
lawns manicured and pesticized
our rooms burdened with the weight
of all the K-Marts, Zellers and Wal-Marts
had to offer
the cycle of earn and spend
constantly renewed.

But before the frantic Consumerism
had lost its magic spell
too soon we heard the dreaded words
Retirement, Pension, R.R.S.P., Condo
reducing all

Achievers, White collar, Professional, Labourer

to one word
Senior

We who in our super-hero climbs
had scorned family, clan, kinship
sunscapes and seascapes
mountain slopes forever green
dotted with majestic pouis
unleashing their pink and yellow blossoms
on a parched and waiting land
bequeathed to us
by our sinned upon and bloodied ancestors
now turn our hearts and eyes
to remembrance of a simpler place
cringing in hope that like the prodigals we are
we will be welcomed back
for smarting from the wounds
inflicted by an alien land
battered and bruised we seek a refuge

the faces of home.

Acknowledgements

The following poems were first published in:

"Roots" and"First Hot Dog" in *Another Way to Dance : Contemporary Asian Poetry from Canada and the United States*, ed. Cyril Dabydeen (Toronto: TSAR Publications, 1996); "The Birth of Roti" in *The Trinidad and Tobago Review*, July 7th, 2003; "Naomi: Woman Lost" in *Contemporary Verse 2*, Winnipeg. Winter, 1993; "Immigrant" in *Other Voices: Writings by Blacks in Canada*, ed. Lorris Elliott (Toronto: Williams-Wallace Publishers, 1985); "Second Migration", "For My Daughter" and "In the Dungeon of My Skin" in *Creation Fire: A CAFRA Anthology of Women's Poetry* , ed Ramabai Espinet (Toronto: Sister Vision Press, 1990); "Invisible Woman" in *Diverse Voices: Manitobans Speak out on Racism.* (Winnipeg: The Coalition for Human Equality, 1996).